FUN FACTS ABOUT ANIMALS

FROM

A TO Z

Illustrated by Sandy Davis / Written by Nina Davis

2016/26/04

A

Arnie, the AARDVARK, lives in Africa and comes out mostly at night to eat cucumbers and ants! Ants... yuck!! How would you like to be an aardvark?

B Bing, the BILLY GOAT, has special eyes that can see almost completely around his head without even turning it. Imagine how much he can see when he actually turns it!

C Carmen, the CAMEL, bats those long eyelashes of hers to protect her eyes from the sand. Camels have a transparent third eyelid called a "haw" that removes sand that gets into their eyes. Pretty cool, huh?

D Donna, the DONKEY, brays like a foghorn when her food is late. **HEE-HAW!** Her cries are so loud, she can be heard almost 2 miles away.

E

Ellie, the ELEPHANT, rolls in the mud to protect her skin from sun and insect bites. You would think she'd be afraid of nothing, but when she sees or hears bees, she runs away and alerts other elephants by making low sounds humans can't hear.

Flora, the FOX, ferrets out insects, birds, eggs and plants to eat. Her thick tail, called a *brush* (it sure looks like one!), helps her keep her balance. It also acts as a warm cover in winter.

G Gillian, The GIRAFFE, gorges herself on green leaves at the top of acacia trees. A cool thing to know is that each giraffe has its own unique coat pattern.

Harry, the HIPPOPOTAMUS, lives in Africa and is mostly herbivorous – that means he eats mainly grasses and plants. Are you surprised to hear his closest relatives are whales and dolphins? We were!

I Iris, the IRISH WOLFHOUND, is well liked because she is loyal, affectionate, and devoted to those she loves and, though she is an excellent hunting dog, what we like best about her is that she is friendly.

J Jack, the JACKRABBIT, looks like a large rabbit but he's really a hare. Unlike rabbits, baby hares are born with their fur on and eyes open and they can take care of themselves soon after being born.

K Kyle, the kookie-looking KOALA, sleeps about 20 hours a day and eats Eucalyptus leaves at night. He may be cute but we wouldn't want to spend that much time sleeping, would you?

Lincoln, the LION, is the second largest in the cat family. He protects the little lion cubs while their mothers do most of the hunting because they are smaller, faster, and don't have his heavy mane. They all live together in a group called a "pride".

M

Molly, the mischievous MONKEY, lives with her "troop" or "tribe" and they work together to take care of the baby monkeys. They live in trees, all play together, and love to cuddle and protect each other.

N Nanette, the NUMBAT, only lives in Western Australia. She has a long tongue with sticky saliva to catch termites. She sure eats a lot of them, up to 20,000 a day!! We love the white stripes on her back. Isn't her coat pretty?

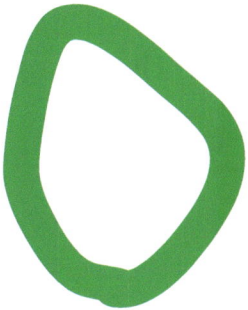

Octavia, the OCELOT, lives in South America and has great eyesight, she even sees well at night. Because of the unique markings on her fur, she's also called a painted leopard. Unlike most cats, she is a good swimmer. What about you?

P Pete, the PIG, has an excellent sense of smell. He uses his long snout to poke underground for food. He can drink four to five gallons of water a day! How much water do you drink in a day?

Quinn, the quirky QUOKKA (kwa-ka), is a marsupial who lives in Western Australia. He's about the size of a cat. He likes people and often follows tourists around on Rottnest Island, where most quokkas live.

R Rita, the rapid REINDEER, is called a "caribou" in North America. They say that at one-day old, a reindeer can run faster than an Olympic sprinter! No wonder Santa Claus uses them to pull his sleigh!

Scarlet, the SKUNK, can hear and smell very well but she has terrible eyesight. She uses her stinky weapon as little as she can, because she only has enough for 5 or 6 sprays and a new supply takes up to 10 days to produce. Whew!

Taffy, The TAPIR, looks like a tall pig but he comes from the horse family. He loves to sink down to walk along the bottom of a river or lake and feed. He eats lots! As much as 80 pounds (36 kilograms) of leaves, berries and fruit in a day.

Uriah, the unusual URIAL, is a wild sheep though he looks like a long-legged goat. He lives on grassy slopes beside mountains from Iran to India in Asia. He has large curly horns that sometimes go all the way around to the back of his head.

V Violet, the VICUNA, lives in the Andes Mountains and, even if she is the national animal of Peru, she's quite shy. Her wool is thick and traps warm air near her body so she can live in really cold climates. Wish I had an awesome coat like that!

W

Willy, The WILDEBEEST (will-de-beast), grazes with his herd alongside zebra on the open plains and grasslands of Africa. They listen for alarm signals from baboons warning of lions nearby. We'd want to know if a lion were close by too, wouldn't you?

X

Xavier, the XERUS, looks like a large standing squirrel and that's exactly what he is, an African ground squirrel. Some Xerus are treated like pets in Africa, and are free to run about like house cats. We wonder if he sits still to be petted and purrrrrrr...s!

Y Yuri, the YAK, lives mostly in Tibet with other yaks in a herd that roams high in the mountains, where they graze on grasses in alpine meadows. Her wool is odor resistant. Wow, we'd never have to take a bath if we were like her!

Z

Zack, the ZEBRA, has unusual ears. They tell you his mood. If he's calm, friendly or tense, his ears stand up straight. If he's afraid, his ears slant forward. And when he's angry, they lean backward. Too bad we can't read human ears like that.

Thank you for taking the time to read "Fun Facts About Animals - From A to Z". If you enjoyed it, please consider posting a short review and telling your friends about it. Word of mouth is an author's best friend and much appreciated. Thank you, Nina & Sandy

For a FREE download of a "coloring" version of this book, please go to our website at www.color.sandyandninabooks.com

www.sandyandninabooks.com

Cover Design by Sandra J. Davis. Interior Layout by Jesse Gordon

www.ingramcontent.com/pod-product-compliance
Lightning Source LLC
Chambersburg PA
CBHW040022050426
42452CB00002B/97